Facts About the Red Kangaroo

By Lisa Strattin

© 2016 Lisa Strattin

Facts for Kids Picture Books by Lisa Strattin

Guanaco, Vol 74

Marine Iguana, Vol 75

Giant Squirrel, Vol 76

Mynah Birds, Vol 77

Red Admiral Butterfly, Vol 78

Star Tortoise, Vol 79

Walking Stick Insect, Vol 80

Shoebill Stork, Vol 81

Jaguarundi, Vol 82

Rhesus Macaque, Vol 83

Sign Up for New Release Emails Here

http://lisastrattin.com/subscribe-here

Join the KidCrafts Monthly Program Here

http://KidCraftsByLisa.com

All rights reserved. No part of this book may be reproduced by any means whatsoever without the written permission from the author, except brief portions quoted for purpose of review.

All information in this book has been carefully researched and checked for factual accuracy. However, the author and publisher makes no warranty, express or implied, that the information contained herein is appropriate for every individual, situation or purpose and assume no responsibility for errors or omissions. The reader assumes the risk and full responsibility for all actions, and the author will not be held responsible for any loss or damage, whether consequential, incidental, special or otherwise, that may result from the information presented in this book.

I have relied on my own observations as well as many different sources for this book and I have done my best to check facts and give credit where it is due. In the event that any material is used without proper permission, please contact me so that the oversight can be corrected.

Table of Contents

INTRODUCTION 7
CHARACTERISTICS 9
APPEARANCE 13
LIFE STAGES 15
LIFE SPAN 19
SIZE 19
HABITAT 21
DIET 23
FRIENDS AND ENEMIES 25
SUITABILITY AS PETS 29
PLUSH KANGAROO 32
KIDCRAFTS MONTHLY SUBSCRIPTION PROGRAM 33

INTRODUCTION

The red kangaroo is the largest marsupial in the world. A marsupial is a mammal that gives birth to tiny, hairless, helpless babies. Many female marsupials have a pouch in which they carry their babies as they grow. All female kangaroos, including the red kangaroo, have pouches.

The scientific name of the red kangaroo is Macropus rufus. Macropus means "long foot," and rufus means "red-haired." Red kangaroos use their long feet, strong legs, and muscular tails to leap across the dry grass plains where they live. Red kangaroos are found only on the continent of Australia.

COLOR ME

CHARACTERISTICS

Red kangaroos are mainly active in the evening and at night when it is fairly cool. During the hot daylight hours, they spend most of their time resting. When they are active, they can move at up to 35 miles per hour. Red kangaroos move by jumping, and are able to jump as much as 25 feet in a single leap.

The red kangaroo has very good eyesight and a wide field of vision. It also has good hearing, and has ears that can each move in a full circle. The red kangaroo has very small vocal chords, so it cannot make a wide range of sounds. However, red kangaroos do sometimes make clicking or clucking sounds. They also thump their feet on the ground, although scientists are not sure why. Some scientists think that this may be a warning of danger. Others have suggested that red kangaroos do this to scare off predators.

COLOR ME

Red kangaroos are somewhat social animals, and tend to live in small groups of two to ten individuals. They compete for dominance and for shady spots. Sometimes red kangaroos engage in "boxing." They support themselves with their tails and sweep at each other with their feet. The largest males are normally dominant.

COLOR ME

APPEARANCE

Red kangaroos have short, soft hair that is usually reddish in color. Females often have a blue tint and are sometimes called "blue fliers." The paws and toes are dark, while the tip of the tail is light. The belly is white, and there is a white patch on each side of the head from mouth to ear.

The red kangaroo has a small head with big eyes and ears. It has a long, muscular tail and strong legs, but the arms are short and rarely used.

COLOR ME

LIFE STAGES

The female red kangaroo gives birth to one baby at a time. At birth, the red kangaroo weights just 0.03 ounces, which is about the size of a pea. The baby is called a joey, and it spends the first two months of its life in its mother's pouch, where it drinks her milk.

COLOR ME

By six months of age, the joey has grown fur and can come out of the pouch for short periods of time. The joey spends less and less time in the pouch until around eight months of age. It continues to nurse by putting its head into the pouch until around one year of age. The mother red kangaroo can have a second joey when the first one reaches eight months of age and is living outside of the pouch. She will nurse both at the same time until the older one reaches one year and no longer needs to nurse. In ideal conditions, a mother red kangaroo can give birth to three joeys in two years.

COLOR ME

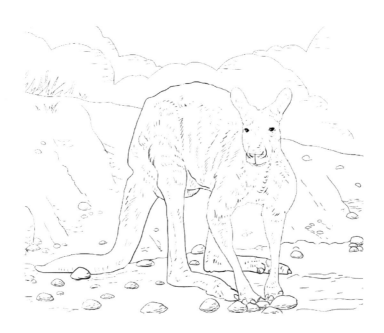

LIFE SPAN

In the wild, red kangaroos live 12-15 years. The longest recorded red kangaroo lifespan is 27 years.

SIZE

The average male red kangaroo stands about 6 ½ feet tall and weighs around 190 pounds. The males are much larger and heavier than the females. The average female is around 4 ½ feet tall and weighs about 80 pounds.

COLOR ME

HABITAT

Red kangaroos live on the dry grass plains of Central Australia. They do not live in the northern part of the continent because the climate is too wet. These animals prefer to stay in areas where there are scattered shade trees. However, they can also be found in shrub land and desert. Red kangaroos have a high tolerance for heat, and stay cool by resting under trees and bushes. They also pant, sweat, and stop exercising when it is hot.

COLOR ME

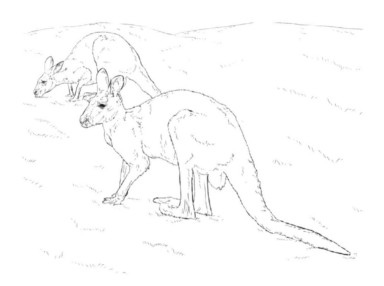

DIET

Red kangaroos are herbivores that eat grass, shrubs, and other plants. When there is a lot of food available, they prefer to stay in one place. When food is scarce, they will travel long distances for food.

COLOR ME

FRIENDS AND ENEMIES

Humans help red kangaroos by rescuing them, providing care, and creating protected spaces. Humans also unintentionally help red kangaroos when clearing land and providing water for livestock. The land and water that humans give to domestic animals are used by red kangaroos. However, humans can sometimes be enemies to the red kangaroo as well.

COLOR ME

Dingoes and humans prey on adult red kangaroos. Foxes and some large birds prey on joeys. Humans hunt red kangaroos for their hides and meat. Humans also threaten red kangaroos in other ways. Over one million red kangaroos are killed each year by cars. However, red kangaroos are not considered endangered or threatened. The current population is estimated to be around 15 million.

COLOR ME

SUITABILITY AS PETS

While some people do breed and keep red kangaroos as pets, this is a bad idea for a number of reasons. First, these animals need a lot more space than most people can provide. Second, red kangaroos cannot be housetrained. Third, they can catch diseases from other household pets. Finally, few vets know much about red kangaroo health. As a result, the death rate among captive domestic red kangaroos is very high.

COLOR ME

Please leave me a review here:

http://lisastrattin.com/Review-Vol-84

For more Kindle Downloads Visit Lisa Strattin Author Page on Amazon Author Central

http://amazon.com/author/lisastrattin

To see upcoming titles, visit my website at LisaStrattin.com – all books available on kindle!

http://lisastrattin.com

PLUSH KANGAROO

You can get one by copying and pasting this link into your browser: **http://lisastrattin.com/PlushKangaroo**

KIDCRAFTS MONTHLY SUBSCRIPTION PROGRAM

Receive a Kids Craft and a Lisa Strattin Full Color Paperback Book Each Month in Your Mailbox!

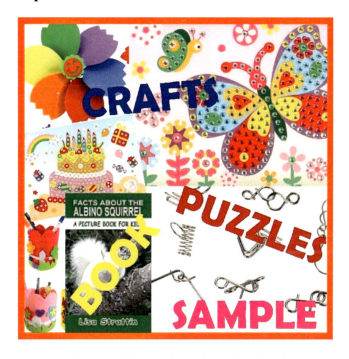

Get yours by copying and pasting this link into your browser

http://KidCraftsByLisa.com